INTRODUCTION

In April of 1991, President George Bush and U.S. Secretary of Education Lamar Alexander announced their education agenda, AMERICA 2000. Immediately, the American Association of School Administrators expressed its appreciation for this added attention to education in our nation.

Shortly thereafter, the AASA Executive Committee approved formation of a blue ribbon panel of education leaders to discuss AMERICA 2000. The panel was charged with recommending formal positions and identifying alternative policies on a number of issues raised by the President's agenda.

AASA's Blue Ribbon Panel on AMERICA 2000 convened in June of 1991. After thoughtful and positive discussion, the group posed questions, issued cautions, tested ideas, made recommendations, and helped to bring into focus a view of what American education can and should become.

The association urges school administrators, board members, teachers, parents, and community leaders to use this important publication as a basis for discussion of AMERICA 2000. AASA challenges school leaders and their communities to develop, when and where appropriate, strategies for implementation. At the same time, AASA urges the President, secretary of education, members of Congress, governors, state legislators, and other elected and appointed government officials to consider where school leaders stand.

Of course, AASA is grateful to the President and secretary of education for their growing interest in schools. They, too, must be part of the education team if the national goals and the intent of AMERICA 2000 are to be realized. We share their commitment to bringing about significant improvements in American education. In fact, we urge the President to go a step further in developing a shared vision for our nation. From that shared vision, our schools can take an even more decisive lead.

As school reform moves forward, the views of local school leaders, without exception, must be thoughtfully considered. It is, after all, in each community that education improvement will actually take place.

We believe the views expressed in this publication will contribute to even better education for the people of our nation.

Richard D. Miller
Executive Director
American Association of School Administrators

Ministry of Education, Ontario
Information Services
13th Floor, Mowat Block, Queen's Park
Toronto   M7A 1L2

HOW TO USE THIS PUBLICATION

AMERICA 2000...Where School Leaders Stand is designed as a basis for school, school system, and community-wide discussions of the President's education strategies. We suggest:

- Obtaining copies of the publication for all staff and involved community leaders.

- Asking that PTAs, advisory groups, and various community organizations review this publication and discuss both AASA's position statements and the questions raised.

- Formulating educational and public responses to the President's strategies.

- Using ideas generated in this publication and through discussions as the basis for newsletter and newspaper articles, speeches, and other forms of communication.

A VIEW OF EDUCATION AMERICA!

The word America itself inspires both the intellect and the emotions. From sea to shining sea, the United States of America has become the capital of democracy and a symbol of freedom. This remarkable nation has also become a magnet that has attracted millions of immigrants who have come seeking renewed inspiration and hope.

Sustaining and nurturing America—ensuring its democratic way of life and its free market economy—has become a monumental challenge as we approach the conclusion of what many have called, "The American Century." A consensus has formed around the idea that education is the very engine of a democracy and the key to our future.

THE EDUCATION SOLUTION

Whenever the nation is challenged—technologically, socially, politically, or economically—we, as a people, have turned to education for solutions and directions. Today, America is facing challenges on all fronts, and again the nation's schools are squarely in the spotlight.

Educators take these challenges seriously. However, they are often frustrated in their efforts to improve education by worsening social and economic conditions affecting children and youth and by shortfalls in state revenues that push them into staff layoffs and a sea of red ink. The degree of difficulty is, in fact, rising in almost direct proportion to our country's expectations. Yet our schools persevere. The examples of excellence abound. Unfortunately, progress is often inhibited by conditions and eclipsed by problems that schools will never be able to solve alone.

Effective schools have at least one thing in common: sound leadership. School administrators have never had a more crucial role in American society; they must be the ones who stimulate the debate and help form a vision of what our schools should become in communities across the nation.

The time has come to agree on what we expect of our schools. Are they institutions that prepare people for the world of work? Are they the cradle of good citizenship? Are they expected to contribute to even more stimulating and personally fulfilling lives? The answer to each of these questions is a resounding yes!

America's schools should also be driven by a deep-seated commitment to developing the individual talents and meeting the individual needs of students. Those students bring to their schools a virtual rainbow of cultures, races, and social and economic conditions. Perhaps no American values are more important than equity and equal opportunity for all.

THE INTERNATIONAL CHALLENGE

Our nation is now enduring shock therapy. During the past few decades, we have nudged toward a conclusion that the goose will not automatically continue to lay golden eggs. Competition from the Pacific Rim, including Japan and Korea, has jolted the business community and the American economy. Now, our nation faces the competition of an emerging European Economic Community. In short, our schools must prepare students to live, work, and lead in a society that is increasingly global. Diplomacy, conflict-resolution, innovation, and communication may be among our most important skills, if they aren't already.

Productivity in many other nations has increased, while American productivity has dipped. This decline has led to diminished income for the middle class whose members are becoming more and more concerned about their children's future and even more fervent in their demand for good education. Economist Anthony Carnavale continues to remind us that a major factor in productivity is the education of the work force. Carnavale also makes clear that even the best education cannot cure economic problems caused by poor management in business and industry.

The time has come to agree on what we expect of our schools.

COLLABORATION IS ESSENTIAL

Collaboration is the word for the 90s. While each segment of society seems intent on blaming the other for America's problems, the time has come for all who are concerned about America's future to sit at the same table. Business and education leaders must communicate with each other, regularly and often.

Organizations that serve children and youth, parents, and educators at all levels must collaborate and form partnerships for the benefit of the client — the student.

Those who serve on the education team must also reach for even greater levels of collaboration. Whether school restructuring leads to what some term school-based management or simply greater collaboration among teachers, administrators, and school boards, to name a few, one thing is certain: The energies currently used in fueling adversary relationships must be redirected toward positive, synergistic accomplishments on behalf of all students to ensure even greater levels of achievement.

In the health arena, collaboration among community organizations may ultimately reach its zenith. Most agree that young people need a sense of self-esteem, adequate diet, physical exercise, immunizations, and knowledge of how to avoid diseases such as AIDS. Physical and mental health are, after all, the foundations of personal and intellectual development.

THE CONDITION OF OUR CHILDREN

No institution has changed more rapidly and dramatically, and with such devastating effect, as the family. Many children today come to school bearing the scars of failed family relationships, the physical and mental bruises of child abuse, and a lack of love and encouragement. In contrast, others have positive experiences and sound supportive relationships that serve as a bedrock for further learning. The gap between the two groups of students is widening and, correspondingly, the challenges for schools are increasing.

In the future, schools and parents must work even more closely for the benefit of each and every student. Adversarial relationships must be replaced by cooperation and communication. Classes in parenting skills and child development for adults may become as common as reading and math as we move into the 21st century.

> *Adversarial relationships must be replaced by cooperation and communication.*

THE ISSUE OF LEARNING

All students can learn. While their interests and learning capacities may vary, their need, desire, and drive to learn is constant. Schools are challenged to ensure that the curriculum is driven by what students need to know and be able to do. Testing and assessment should be designed to measure actual progress and guide the learning process, not simply to serve as a scoreboard to pit school against school or to praise or humiliate educators.

Learning should be lifelong. It should never stop. A late bloomer might catch intellectual fire at age 20 or age 85. Whenever there is a yearning to learn, our education system should be ready to contribute, whether that learning is geared toward personal fulfillment or advancing or changing careers.

ENTER AMERICA 2000

AMERICA 2000 is more than a report or strategy. It is a phenomenon that provides an opportunity to continue the debate and to rethink the priorities and structures that now characterize the nation's schools.

The question is not whether America's schools have done a remarkable job—they have. The question is not how to correct what has gone wrong. The question is: How can we make our schools more effective in preparing students for a fast-changing world?

The President's proposals deserve careful and constructive review. Every thoughtful American should ask a number of questions about the White House recommendations, including the following:

- What type of future can our children expect?

- What is included here that could actually help achieve a better education and a brighter future for every student?

- How much of AMERICA 2000 promotes a narrow political agenda that could actually damage public education?

- What is missing from this set of proposals, and what does the answer to this question tell us about how well or how poorly the challenges facing education are understood and addressed?

- How can schools and communities get together to study AMERICA 2000 and deal with its recommendations?

> AMERICA 2000 ... It is a phenomenon that provides an opportunity to continue the debate and to rethink the priorities and structures that now characterize the nation's schools.

A FOUR-PART STRATEGY

AMERICA 2000 is a four-part strategy. Those parts include:

1. For today's students, we must radically improve today's schools, all 110,000 of them—make them better and more accountable for results.

2. For tomorrow's students, we must invent new schools to meet the demands of a new century—a New Generation of American Schools, bringing at least 535 of them into existence by 1996 and thousands by decade's end.

3. For those of us already out of school and in the work force, we must keep learning if we are to live and work successfully in today's world. A "Nation at Risk" must become a "Nation of Students."

4. For schools to succeed, we must look beyond their classrooms to our communities and families. Schools will never be much better than the commitment of their communities. Each of our communities must become a place where learning can happen.

AMERICA 2000'S CORE CURRICULUM

AMERICA 2000 focuses on a core curriculum consisting of five subjects: English, mathematics, science, history, and geography.

THE NATIONAL EDUCATION GOALS

AMERICA 2000 strategies come on the heels of a series of six national goals for education, developed at a 1989 summit involving the President, White House staff, and governors. That summit, which excluded groups such as educators and the U.S. Congress, hammered out the following goals which were unveiled in the President's January 1990 State of the Union address:

By the year 2000 —

- All children in America will start school ready to learn.
- The high school graduation rate will increase to at least 90 percent.
- American students will leave grades 4, 8, and 12 having demonstrated competency in challenging subject matter, including English, mathematics, science, history, and geography; and every school in America will ensure that all students learn to use their minds well, so they may be prepared for responsible citizenship, further learning, and productive employment in our modern economy.
- U.S. students will be first in the world in science and mathematics achievement.
- Every adult American will be literate and will possess the knowledge and skills necessary to compete in a global economy and exercise the rights and responsibilities of citizenship.
- Every school in America will be free of drugs and violence and will offer a disciplined environment conducive to learning.

These goals have been endorsed by numerous education leadership organizations, including AASA.

Numerous school leaders have expressed concern that the AMERICA 2000 strategies come up short and that real reform must go far beyond the President's proposals. Many are puzzled by the fact that the arts, health, and programs to sustain citizenship are missing. Still others cannot understand the lack of alignment with the national goals. For example, school readiness, firmly ensconced in the national goals, didn't make it into the AMERICA 2000 initiative.

Some question what AMERICA 2000 says, some what it doesn't say, and others what it should say.

ISSUES RAISED BY AMERICA 2000

The panel of education leaders convened by AASA to explore AMERICA 2000 posed numerous questions and contributed to the development of several position statements.

Twelve AMERICA 2000 recommendations are explored in the following pages. The last is the issue of what is missing from the President's education agenda.

1. NEW AMERICAN SCHOOLS

What AMERICA 2000 Recommends: "Each AMERICA 2000 Community may develop a plan to create one of the first 535+ New American Schools with limited federal support for start-up costs. In the plan, they will be expected to suggest their own answer to the question: What would it take to develop the best school in the world in this community, a school that serves the children of this community, also meeting the national goals? At least one New American School will be created in each congressional district by 1996. Congress will be asked to provide one-time grants of $1 million to each of the first 535+ New American Schools to cover start-up costs. (The grants, as proposed, would be for a three-year period.) State, local, and private resources will enable thousands more such schools to begin by the end of the decade.

"The mission of the research and development teams is to help communities create schools that will reach the national education goals, including World Class Standards (in all five core subjects, identified as English, mathematics, science, history, and geography) for all students, as monitored by the American Achievement Tests and similar measures. Once the R&D is complete and the schools are launched, the operating costs of the New American Schools will be about the same as those of conventional schools."

Where We Stand: The development of at least 535+ New American Schools as demonstration sites is unlikely to transform the other 99.5 percent of U.S. public schools in a time frame that will meet the nation's needs. However, pilot sites can be instructive, provided all public schools have equal opportunity to be selected. The federal government should guarantee that those schools represent the diversity of the nation and that the selections are based on a rigorous, competitive, but reasonable process, completely separated from political considerations. A plan should be developed to guarantee that what is learned through these sites, as well as currently successful practices in other schools, will be broadly shared. Short-term demonstrations are not a substitute for long-term positive and constructive change.

Questions To Answer/Issues To Discuss:
- How will schools without grant-writing capacity be able to effectively compete with those that do?
- Will the review process be rigorous and competitive and not political, since the schools would be placed in each congressional district?
- How can the federal government continue to say no more funding is needed for schools when a primary recommendation is to provide an additional $1 million for each of the schools selected?
- Is the New American School a Trojan Horse providing cover for the introduction of choice programs?
- Does the added $1 million for each New American School and the possible relaxation of inhibiting laws, rules, and regulations make the school so atypical that others will not be able to emulate its successes?
- Does the placement of one New American School in each area served by a member of Congress actually limit the effectiveness of the model since the best candidates for demonstration sites may not be that evenly distributed?
- What will happen to funding for these demonstration schools after three years when the $1 million runs out? Are states, communities, and the federal government prepared to provide the dollars to sustain them and to spread what has been learned to all schools?
- Will a school system have to commit itself to supporting long-term systemic change to have

> Short-term demonstrations are not a substitute for long-term positive and constructive change.

a school selected as a demonstration site?
- Will the research and development done in preparation for the New American Schools program be reinforced by a substantial state and federal investment in related professional development for teachers and administrators?
- Will selected schools be required to educate all students rather than select only the most motivated or expel those who are hardest to educate?
- Will equal opportunity and accessibility be as basic to the New American Schools as to existing public schools?
- Will schools that are selected reflect the diversity of the country and its schools?
- Will the thousands of excellent programs currently working in schools across the nation be broadly shared along with the experiences of the demonstration sites?
- How will state and national education leadership organizations, local school leaders, colleges and universities, service agencies, study councils, research organizations, and various consortia be involved in defining and contributing to the success of the effort?

2. WORLD CLASS STANDARDS

What AMERICA 2000 recommends: "Standards will be developed, in conjunction with the National Education Goals Panel. These World Class Standards — for each of the five core subjects — will represent what young Americans need to know and be able to do if they are to live and work successfully in today's world. These standards will incorporate both knowledge and skills to ensure that, when they leave school, young Americans are prepared for further study and the work force.

"Definitions of what American students should be expected to know and be able to do upon completion of schooling (are) meant to function as benchmarks against which students and school performance can be measured."

Where We Stand: World Class Standards can be an important step on the road to maintaining America's competitive position in the world. Those standards, however, should reflect the uniquenesses of the American people and what the people of our nation need to know and be able to do to sustain a democracy and free-market economy, as well as to achieve high levels of self-sufficiency and personal fulfillment. The vision of the future assumed by World Class Standards must be widely shared and reflect ownership by a broad cross-section of the American people, in addition to educators.

Standards should not be limited only to areas of education that are easily tested and compared. In addition, any standards should be accompanied by the resources and commitment to help all students reach them and should not lead to increases in failure or dropout rates.

Questions To Answer/Issues To Discuss:
- What is a "World Class Standard?" Are there both outcome standards and process standards?
- Who will decide what these standards should be? Who will be involved in the process?
- Will the standards be appropriate to the current and future needs of students and society?
- Will these standards lead to invidious labeling of students?
- How can or will these standards encourage improvements in teaching?
- How can we be sure these standards will include those areas of education not easily tested or compared with performance of students in other nations?
- How will we ensure high standards for all, not only the students who traditionally achieve at the highest levels?
- Is our nation prepared, at all levels, to provide the help and resources that will support students in reaching those standards?
- Does the federal government plan to make these standards a top priority and commit additional resources to them?

> ...any standards should be accompanied by the resources and commitment to help all students reach them and should not lead to increases in failure or dropout rates.

3. AMERICAN ACHIEVEMENT TESTS

What AMERICA 2000 Recommends: "In conjunction with the National Education Goals Panel, a new (voluntary) nationwide examination system will be developed, based on the five core subjects, tied to the World Class Standards. These tests will be designed to foster good teaching and learning, as well as to monitor student progress.

"Report Cards on Results: More than reports on how their children are doing, these report cards will also provide clear (and comparable) public information on how schools, school dis-

ISSUES RAISED BY AMERICA 2000

tricts, and states are doing, as well as the entire nation. The national and state report cards will be prepared in conjunction with the National Education Goals Panel.

"Congress will be asked to authorize the National Assessment of Educational Progress regularly to collect state-level data in grades 4, 8, and 12 in all five core subjects, beginning in 1994. Congress will also be asked to permit the use of National Assessment results at district and school levels by states that wish to do so."

Where We Stand: Some leaders in the federal government, and certain others, are currently intent on further national testing. However, what is truly required is improvement in individual assessments that will help teachers and schools improve education for each child. A scoreboard mentality has developed that undermines efforts aimed at enhancing student achievement. Any testing program must recognize the needs of students to do their own personal best and achieve their personal goals, not just enhance comparisons with other schools, school districts, groups, states, or nations. In addition, a testing program should recognize the importance of both growth and overall performance. It should not be used to penalize either schools or students struggling against severe social and economic hardships. In this nation, any national test should reflect the needs of society and include an assessment of thinking, problem-solving, and interpersonal skills — areas of testing not yet fully developed. Of course, all tests of any type should be fairly and efficiently administered.

> *A* scoreboard mentality has developed that undermines efforts aimed at enhancing student achievement.

Questions To Answer/Issues To Discuss:
- Will these American Achievement Tests force a national curriculum, putting the cart before the horse?
- What is most important for students, doing their personal best and reaching their personal goals or devoting their school careers to being competitive on a national test?
- How will these tests, and ultimately the curriculum, be protected from the political whims of the party or individuals currently holding office?
- Will these tests result in further honors for the haves and further pointing up the inadequacies of the have-nots?

- What will be done to provide essential resources for those schools and students that do not score well on these tests?
- Will these tests further add to the nation's scoreboard mentality and distract from forms of testing and assessment that yield much more useful information for improving education for each student?
- How will the federal government coordinate this program with others it is sponsoring to recognize schools, such as the Merit Schools program?
- Will the program recognize both progress and performance, or will it provide greatest honors to those who already have adequate resources and accompanying performance and penalize those who don't?

4. GOVERNORS' ACADEMIES FOR TEACHERS AND SCHOOL LEADERS

What AMERICA 2000 Recommends: "Academies will be established with federal seed money, so that principals and other leaders in every state will be able to make their schools better and more accountable.

"Academies will also be established with federal seed money, so that teachers of the five core subjects in every state will be ready to help their students attain the World Class Standards and pass the American Achievement Tests."

Where We Stand: Professional development is essential for central office and building-level administrators, teachers, and other school personnel. A significant investment in professional development has great potential value for improving education, provided education leaders at the local, state, and national levels have an opportunity to develop the program, share with each other what already works, and evaluate the effectiveness of the academies. Any professional development program of this type should focus on what is essential to increase learner performance and the payoff for society. It should be continuous, not a one-shot-deal, and should ultimately help people do their jobs better. At their best, these academies would offer opportunities for teachers and administrators to learn together

> *Any professional development program ... should focus on what is essential to increase learner performance and the payoff for society. It should be continuous, not a one-shot-deal, and should ultimately help people do their jobs better.*

in teams and promote system-wide improvement. These Governors' Academies should be free of partisan political influence in the selection of programs or instructors. Ultimately, they should not be seen as a substitute for building the professional development capacities of school systems and the capabilities of colleges and universities to enhance those local efforts.

Questions To Ask/Issues To Discuss:
- Will funding be provided for professional development of both school and school district leaders?
- Will the programs of these academies be influenced by what is learned through research and development and the identified needs of local, state, and national education leaders?
- Will the professional development offered by these academies be driven by the need to improve student outcomes overall and not simply confined to the five core subjects identified by the federal government in AMERICA 2000?
- Will educators and school systems have significant opportunities to share their techniques and successes with each other?
- Will these academies be one-shot-deals, or will they have continuous funding over a long period of time?
- Will these academies enhance or undermine the capacities of school systems and universities to offer professional development?
- Do the Governors' Academies contradict the AMERICA 2000 quest to make the local school the site of reform?
- Since these are Governors' Academies, will individual governors or their staffs be able to include or eliminate certain programs or presenters to reflect certain political views or individual biases?

5. THE SCHOOL AS THE SITE OF REFORM

What AMERICA 2000 Recommends: "Because real education improvement happens school-by-school, the teachers, principals, and parents in each school must be given the authority — and the responsibility — to make important decisions about how the schools will operate. Federal and state red tape that gets in the way needs to be cut. States will be encouraged to allow the leadership of individual schools to make decisions about how resources are used, and Congress will be asked to enact Education Flexibility legislation to remove federal constraints that impede the ability of states to spend education resources most effectively to raise student achievement levels. The Business Roundtable, the U.S. Chamber of Commerce, and other groups representing the private sector are to be commended — and encouraged — in their important efforts to create state and local policy environments in which school-by-school reform can succeed."

Where We Stand: The local school is where formal education takes place. It is a point of both leadership and delivery. School-based management and involvement techniques are essential. However, the reform of a single school is not enough. All schools and school "systems" must constantly strive to do better. Therefore, strong leadership and support from the overall community, school board, superintendent, and central office administrators, working in concert with principals, teachers, parents, and others, are required to build broad support and to ensure the spread of excellence. To quote an African proverb, "It takes an entire village to educate a child."

Questions To Ask/Issues To Discuss:
- Does AMERICA 2000 ignore the vital importance of school system leadership in stimulating individual school reform?
- How can innovations and improvements at the local school level be shared system-wide to strengthen the education of all students?
- What can be done to ensure that the talents and experience of central office administrators who are experts in various aspects of education contribute to the success of school improvement programs?
- How can the community become more engaged in improvement efforts, since it is the community that must ultimately tolerate and sustain any new approaches to education?

> "It takes an entire village to educate a child." — African proverb

6. CHOICE

What AMERICA 2000 Recommends: "If standards, tests, and report cards tell parents and voters how their schools are doing, choice gives them the leverage to act. Such choices should include all schools that serve the public and are accountable to public authority, regardless of who runs them. New incentives will be provided to states and localities to adopt comprehensive choice policies, and the largest federal school aid program (Chapter I) will be revised to ensure that federal dollars follow the child, to whatever extent state and local policies permit."

Where We Stand: School choice creates equity problems and, when extended to parochial schools, violates the Constitutionally-guaranteed separation of church and state. Choice proposals described in AMERICA 2000 are based on flawed reasoning. They assume that some schools will ultimately be good and others bad and that people should choose among them. In fact, education in every school should be excellent, allowing each student access to a challenging curriculum and the opportunity to succeed at his or her highest level. It is unfortunate that the administration has used AMERICA 2000 to sell its political agenda, including choice and the transfer of public funds to private and parochial schools. This proposal alone tends to undermine the credibility of the entire program.

A Note from Public Opinion Research: The American people expressed themselves on the issue of private school choice in the 1991 Gallup Poll on Public Attitudes Toward Public Schools. Sixty-eight percent said they oppose "allowing students and parents to choose a private school to attend at public expense," while only 26 percent favored that approach. That research was confirmed in a recent study completed for the Democratic National Party by Greenberg-Lake, Tarrance and Associates, which indicated that voters reject education choice by a margin of two-to-one.

Questions To Ask/Issues To Discuss:
- Should all schools be excellent or should some remain better than others to sustain the federal administration's choice program?
- Does choice make more sense when students have a variety of quality academic programs to choose from, such as those offered through magnet schools?
- Why does the administration suggest choice programs that will increase equity problems and violate Constitutional requirements governing the separation of church and state?
- Will choice programs ultimately cost more for services not directly related to education, such as transportation?
- Isn't it time that the administration focused on helping schools in their efforts to achieve individual learner success rather than using AMERICA 2000 to sell part of a political agenda?

> *Choice proposals described in AMERICA 2000 are based on flawed reasoning.*

7. DIFFERENTIAL PAY FOR TEACHERS

What AMERICA 2000 Recommends: "Differential pay will be encouraged for those who teach well, who teach core subjects, who teach in dangerous and challenging settings, or who serve as mentors for new teachers."

Where We Stand: Compensation programs, developed locally, should enhance the efforts of schools to attract into education careers the best and brightest in society. Schools must have the latitude to determine rewards for teachers based on market forces, degree of difficulty, time commitment, and leadership requirements. Career ladders, differentiated staffing, and bonuses might also influence the pay of educators. However, compensation plans that promote competition rather than cooperation will stand in the way of system-wide improvement. Ultimately, the ability to attract and reward talent will help school systems keep excellent teachers in the classroom. Conversely, tenure systems should be reviewed to assess whether they enhance or inhibit education improvement.

Questions To Answer/Issues To Discuss:
- Is differential pay for teachers a federal issue? Isn't this issue best addressed at the local level?
- Is further research required on how to best compensate educators?
- How can compensation systems lead to an assurance that we have the very best people teaching our children?

> *Compensation plans that promote competition rather than cooperation will stand in the way of system-wide improvement.*

8. ALTERNATIVE TEACHER AND PRINCIPAL CERTIFICATION

What AMERICA 2000 Recommends: "Congress will be asked to make grants available to states and districts to develop alternative certification systems for teachers and principals. New college graduates and others seeking a career change into teaching or school leadership are often frustrated by certification requirements unrelated to subject area knowledge or leadership ability. This initiative will help states and districts to develop means by which individuals with an interest in and talent for teaching and school leadership can overcome these barriers."

Where We Stand: Both the National Policy Board for Educational Administration and the National Board for Professional Teaching Standards have addressed the issue of alternative teacher and administrator certification. Almost two-thirds of states are estimated to already have alternative certification programs on the books. It is inappropriate to assume that anyone can teach without adequate preparation. Therefore, a greater need is to improve the quality of both preservice and inservice preparation programs for all who become certified as teachers and administrators.

Questions To Ask/Issues To Discuss:
- Two-thirds of the states already have alternative certification programs. Is it, therefore, an issue that should command federal energies and resources?
- Isn't the real answer found in the need to strengthen both preservice and inservice preparation programs for educators?
- Why duplicate the work of the National Board for Professional Teaching Standards and the National Policy Board for Educational Administration, both of which have addressed this issue recently?
- Since many versions of accreditation already exist, is additional research called for before moving ahead?

9. RESEARCH AND DEVELOPMENT

What AMERICA 2000 Recommends:
"America's business leaders will establish — and muster the private resources for — the New American School Development Corporation, a new nonprofit organization that will award contracts in 1992 to three to seven research and development teams. (Currently, the strategy is calling for 15 to 30 design teams from which three to seven designs will eventually be chosen.) These teams may consist of corporations, universities, think tanks, school innovators, management consultants, and others. The President will ask his Education Policy Advisory Committee, as well as the U.S. Department of

> *It is inappropriate to assume that anyone can teach without adequate preparation.*

Education, to examine the work of these R&D teams (and similar break-the-mold school reform efforts), and to report regularly on their progress to him and to the American people."

Where We Stand: Research is as vital to education as it is to any other enterprise. Therefore, we support research efforts tied to needs identified with the involvement of local, state, and national education leaders. Since the federal government already provides multi-million dollar support for research through the Office of Educational Research and Improvement and several education laboratories, further coordination will be required to avoid duplication of effort. These R&D efforts should ultimately be supported through federal dollars, allowing businesses to continue to make more targeted contributions to schools and the education enterprise.

Questions To Ask/Issues To Discuss:
- Will the federal government consider significant research that has already taken place or is being conducted? While R&D are vital, the federal government is already spending $30 million a year on its R&D centers. What are we learning from them? How do they fit in? Is the process working?
- How will the necessary research and evaluation for the implementation and effectiveness of the New American Schools be supported?
- Shouldn't R&D for education be funded by government instead of business?
- Will these research teams listen to the requirements of practitioners in the field in developing their research agendas?

> Research is as vital to education as it is to any other enterprise.

10. A COMMUNITY WHERE LEARNING CAN HAPPEN

What AMERICA 2000 Recommends: AMERICA 2000 Communities (are) communities, designated by the governors, that meet the President's four-part challenge: that (1) adopt the six national education goals for themselves, (2) create a community-wide plan for achieving them, (3) develop a report card to measure their progress, and (4) demonstrate their readiness to create and support a New American School. 535+ such communities will open New American Schools by 1996.

"The President believes that it is essential to reaffirm such enduring values as personal responsibility, individual action, and other core principles that must underpin life in a democratic society. The aim of the AMERICA 2000 Community Campaign is to make our communities places where learning can happen."

Where We Stand: A campaign in support of better education should take place in every community across America. Those campaigns, based on collaboration among numerous community groups, should consider the need for school readiness, the physical and mental health of children and youth, prenatal care for expectant mothers, improved ethical examples the community provides for its children, better problem-solving and other life skills, deeper knowledge of and commitment to good citizenship, a more thorough understanding of the requirement for lifelong learning, building greater support for schools, and continuously making education more effective. The federal government should set an example for collaboration and caring by working directly with the education community, becoming more sensitive to the social and economic problems affecting youth, and supporting establishment of a Children's Investment Trust, which would provide the equivalent of a social security system for children.

Questions To Ask/Issues To Discuss:
- Since school readiness is not addressed in these strategies, should it be acknowledged here?
- Would it be a good idea to encourage collaboration among all community agencies that serve children, youth, and families, including the schools? If so, how can schools establish themselves among the groups that begin and sustain these types of activities?
- If the administration is serious about AMERICA 2000, how can it continue to give short shrift to the social and economic problems affecting youth?
- Should business offer further incentives for students who stay in school, since many young people lose hope as they explore job prospects? Should business base hiring decisions on student performance and behavior in school?

> *The federal government should set an example for collaboration and caring by working directly with the education community ...*

11. BRINGING AMERICA ON LINE

What AMERICA 2000 Recommends: "The secretary (of education), in consultation with the President's science advisor and the director of the National Science Foundation, will convene a group of experts to help determine how one or more electronic networks might be designed to provide the New American Schools with ready access to the best of information, research, instructional materials and educational expertise. The New American School R&D teams will be asked for their recommendations on the same question. These networks may eventually serve all American schools as well as homes, libraries, colleges, and other sites where learning occurs."

Where We Stand: A network connecting AMERICA 2000 Schools with each other and with other networks providing valuable information is a sound idea. The infrastructure for a national network already exists through federally supported projects such as the ERIC Clearinghouse. Numerous other networks serving education are also already on line. This proposal should be expanded to address the need for schools to increase their access to and use of various types of educational technology to improve learning, including but not limited to telecommunications and video discs. This strategy lacks essential ingredients — the need for teachers to use technology in generating better information about their students and the instructional materials available to meet student learning needs. Making full use of technology in every school system will require a massive new commitment of resources.

Questions To Ask/Issues To Discuss:
- How should this proposal fit into existing computer networks?
- How can schools raise the resources to give teachers access to telephones that are often the gateway to the use of new technologies?
- How does this proposal fit with Congressional initiatives to create systems of "electronic highways?"
- While this type of sharing would be useful, isn't it a very narrow view of technology needed by schools?

> *Making full use of technology in every school system will require a massive new commitment of resources.*

12. FOR THE REST OF US

What AMERICA 2000 Recommends: "Eighty-five percent of America's work force for the year 2000 is already in the work force today, so improving schools for today's and tomorrow's students is not enough to assure a competitive America in 2000. And we need more than job skills to live well in America today. We need to learn more to become better parents, neighbors, citizens, and friends. Education is not just about making a living; it is also about making a life.

"That is why the President is challenging adult Americans to go back to school and make this a 'nation of students.' For our children to understand the importance of their own education, we must demonstrate that learning is important to grown-ups, too. We must ourselves 'go back to school.' The President is urging every American to continue learning throughout his or her life, using the myriad of formal and informal means available to gain further knowledge and skills."

Where We Stand: We agree that the education of those already in the work force and those who have already undertaken the responsibilities of parenthood should not be ignored. Job training and retraining, skills clinics, literacy programs, parent education, and education programs that will reinforce the intellectual skills of our people are vital to the nation's future. Of course, learning should be lifelong, from the cradle to the grave, with ample allowance for prenatal care that contributes to the future physical and emotional health of a child.

> *Learning should be lifelong ... with ample allowance for prenatal care ...*

Questions To Ask/Issues To Discuss:
- What further work should be done to ensure that all Americans understand the importance and payoffs of education throughout their lives?
- What needs to be done to ensure access to quality learning opportunities for people of all ages?
- What can be done to increase the demand and support for parent education programs?

13. WHAT'S BEEN LEFT OUT?

While AMERICA 2000 addresses a number of important issues, it has left out or treated lightly some very important education concerns.

Those who expected this agenda to align with the previously adopted and widely accepted national goals for education have been somewhat disappointed. For example, school readiness, the first goal identified by the President and the nation's governors, receives little or no attention in AMERICA 2000.

Among the most glaring omissions is any discussion of the federal role in dealing with the worsening social and economic conditions affecting children and youth. Many make the case that the federal government's neglect has contributed substantially to these problems which are overwhelming many states and local communities. Equity concerns also take a back seat in AMERICA 2000. In fact, a case can be made that some recommendations, such as the one for expansion of choice, will even worsen the equity challenge and lead to church-state entanglements.

AMERICA 2000 focuses most of its academic attention on five core subjects, leaving out the need for thinking and decision-making skills, the arts, citizenship education, vocational education, the study of other cultures, foreign languages, and so on. Governance is barely mentioned. Accountability is passed off as testing. Issues such as the need to enhance the schools' use of technology to improve learning are shortchanged. While research is a key component in the strategies, how an ongoing research agenda will be developed and the depth of commitment is unclear.

The discussion of funding is confined to New American Schools. If we hope to move schools toward greater success in educating students, then the federal government should fully fund Head Start, Chapter I, and other vital programs. A nation that can raise more than $500 billion to bail out its savings and loans and ready a massive military force in a short period of time should be able to contribute more substantially to improving its schools, which are the best investment we can make in the future of our nation.

> *Among the most glaring omissions is any discussion of the federal role in dealing with the worsening social and economic conditions affecting children and youth.*

A CALL FOR PRESIDENTIAL LEADERSHIP: The President has already taken a lead in the establishment of education goals for the nation. Now, our schools need his leadership and support in gathering resources and making public policy changes that will support local schools and school systems in the achievement of those goals.

We call upon the President to take a further lead in developing a shared vision of the nation and the world we'd like to see for all of today's and tomorrow's children. Then, education can align itself to that vision.

CONTINUE THE DISCUSSION

We hope this booklet, *AMERICA 2000...Where School Leaders Stand*, will contribute to lively discussions about the President's agenda and other education issues. Together, educators and the communities they serve should continue the discussion and keep education high on the American agenda. Our future depends on it.

ACKNOWLEDGMENTS

The American Association of School Administrators is grateful to the following members of its Blue Ribbon Panel on AMERICA 2000:

- **Jack Anderson,** superintendent, East Ramapo Central Schools, Spring Valley, New York

- **Louis Esparo,** superintendent, Pomperaug Regional School District 15, Middlebury, Connecticut

- **Philip Geiger,** superintendent, Piscataway Township Public Schools, New Jersey

- **Willis Hawley,** director, Center for Educational Policy, Peabody College, Vanderbilt University, Nashville, Tennessee

- **Mary Jarvis,** principal, Smoky Hill High School, Cherry Creek School District, Aurora, Colorado

- **Eugene Karol,** superintendent, Calvert County Schools, Prince Frederick, Maryland

- **Roger Kaufman,** professor and director of the Center for Needs Assessment and Planning, Florida State University, Tallahassee, Florida

- **Lee Etta Powell,** former superintendent, Cincinnati Public Schools, Ohio

- **Roberta Stanley,** executive assistant for state and federal relations, Michigan Department of Education, Lansing, Michigan

CONTINUE THE DISCUSSION

AMERICA 2000...Where School Leaders Stand was reviewed and approved by the AASA Executive Committee, whose members include: President William Morris, Vice President Robert Fox, President-Elect Paul Jung, Past-President Erling Clausen, Wayne Blevins, Wayne Doyle, John Duncan, Lewis Finch, Roland Haun, Chuck McKenna, Lee Etta Powell, and Joan Stipetic.

Senior Associate Executive Director for External Services Bruce Hunter formed and led discussions of the AASA Blue Ribbon Panel. Senior Associate Executive Director for Communications Gary Marx wrote and edited the manuscript and responded to suggestions from both the panel and Executive Committee. Executive Director Richard Miller served as project initiator and counselor. AASA Director of Communications Luann Fulbright oversaw the book's production.

> Ministry of Education, Ontario
> Information Services
> 13th Floor, Mowat Block, Queen's Park
> Toronto   M7A 1L2

AMERICAN
ASSOCIATION
OF SCHOOL
ADMINISTRATORS

1801 N. MOORE STREET
ARLINGTON, VA 22209